FAMILY, THE DEPRESSION & BUZZ BOMBS OVER LONDON: ONE LIFE FROM THE GREATEST GENERATION

FAMILY, THE DEPRESSION & BUZZ BOMBS OVER LONDON: ONE LIFE FROM THE GREATEST GENERATION

By Grover Cleveland Futch, Jr.

INTERVIEW
You™

Published by Interview You
Athens, Georgia
www.interviewyou.net

Interview conducted by Keating McCarthy

*The 1928 Ford logo reproduced herein is a
registered trademark of Ford Motor Company.*

*On the cover: G. C. Futch, Jr., at age twenty in Wiesbaden,
Germany, in 1945, the Twelfth U. S. Army Group.*

ISBN 0-9773365-5-7
Printed in the United States of America

This short version of my life is dedicated to the following:

*To my wife, Mildred, for over fifty-seven years of love, devotion,
and encouragement;*

*To my children Greg and Diane, of whom I am really proud, not only for the
things they have accomplished in their professional lives, but also for the high
standards they have set and maintained in their personal lives;*

To all my grandchildren for the joy they have brought to my life;

To my sister Mary, who shared in many of these experiences prior to 1943;

*To my son-in-law, Darryl, and my daughter-in-law, Penny, for
their unwavering support;*

*To my deceased daughter, Barbara, of whom I have often wondered over
the past fifty years what might have been had she lived;*

*To my deceased parents who, I now understand, did the best they
could when faced with unbelievably hard times;*

To my deceased older brothers and sisters, who survived these same experiences;

*To my many nieces and nephews who would get a "kick" out of many
of the things related here;*

*And last, but certainly not least, to the entire Mercer family for accepting
me, for supporting me, for loving me and making me one of their own
for the last fifty-eight years.*

Contents

G. C. Futch, Jr., reaching over to his sister Mary in late 1926 or early 1927

CHAPTER 1

G.C.

My name is Grover C. Futch, Jr. The *C* stands for Cleveland. My father was named for the president and I was named for him. I'm the Junior. The Senior was born in 1897 when Grover Cleveland was president. I've been called everything, but most people call me by my initials: "G. C." I was born in 1924, the sixth of eight children born to Grover Cleveland Futch, Sr., and Frances Esther Shuman in Bryan County, Georgia, which is down near the coast—near Savannah. I was born at my grandmother Shuman's house. My mother had gone to visit her parents. She already had five youngsters. Why she went so far into her pregnancy, I'll never know. But, while she was there,

I came along. It was in the middle of the night, and she had a younger brother who was still at home, my Uncle Earl. He had a Model "T" Ford, so he got up in the middle of the night and went to get the doctor. He said it was raining and it was cool, but the doctor arrived and I came along.

So at that time we lived in Savannah. My father was one of eighteen children born to John and Elizabeth Futch from Bulloch County. My mother had come up from an area called Downs Town. That's where she grew up. My mother was one of five children born to Joe and Mary Shuman. My grandmother's maiden name was Downs, and she inherited a farm through her father, who settled the whole area originally. So we lived in Savannah, and I had another sister born two years later.

In about 1920–21, my father became employed by the Savannah Transit Company as a conductor on a streetcar. At that time, the streetcars ran on rails with a thing that went up to an electric wire, and he was a motorman-conductor. I remember that, and I can remember that there were times when he would take some of us with him to work and let us ride on the streetcar up on the first seat, right near him. If we got to the end of the line—a streetcar, you can drive it from either end—he would change around and we'd go to the other end and sit near him. I remember clearly that he would take my older sister—just older than I so that if I was four, she would be six—and I both to ride with him sometimes. At some point, he lost his job; I don't know why. Maybe it was cutbacks due to hard times, but I heard my mother say it was partly due to his being caught drinking on the job. That's when things went downhill. First, though, some family background.

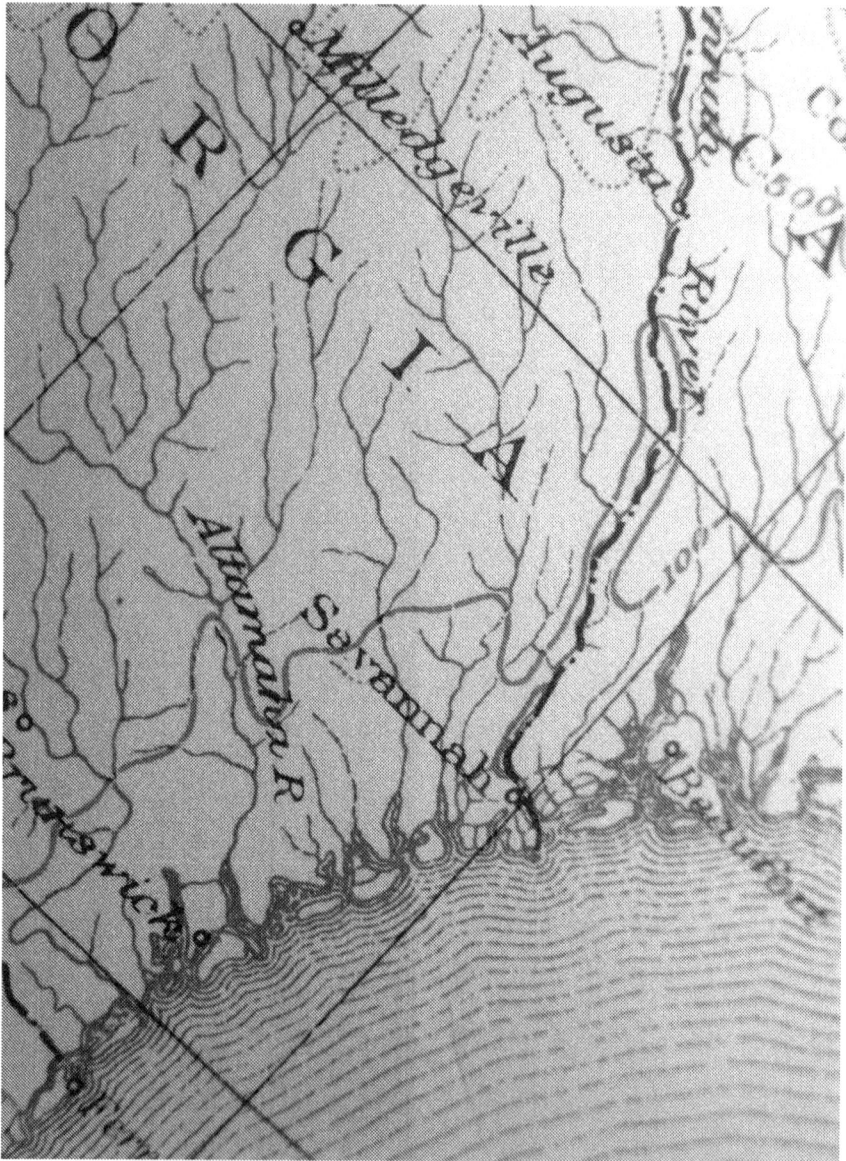

CHAPTER 2

Grandma Shuman

My Grandma Shuman never lived with us. She had her own family and she lived in Downs Town, which was way out in the country. I always liked to go there when I was growing up because she always had a lot of good things to eat. There were hams in the smokehouse and sausage, all that kind of stuff. Grandma Shuman was a remarkable woman. She not only worked on the farm and did all this canning of fruits and vegetables in the summer, but she also raised her children, her grandchildren, and a great-grandchild.

My mother's oldest sister and her husband both died of typhoid fever some years after they were married, and left one small girl, Willie Mae. My grandma Shuman took Willie Mae and raised her. Willie Mae married a man whose last name was also Shuman, and they had a little girl, Ruby. As I understand it, Willie Mae's husband was cruel to her and the child. Grandma Shuman convinced Willie Mae and Ruby to leave, so she and Ruby were taken back to Grandma and Grandpa Shuman. It is ironic, but Willie Mae also took typhoid fever and died when Ruby was about four or five years old. I can still remember today driving in the car from Savannah to attend her funeral.

So my grandmother Shuman raised her great-grandchild as well. My uncle, her oldest son, was a complete alcoholic, and gave them nothing but trouble with his drinking. He divorced his wife, and my grandmother took two of his sons, Jack and Bernice. She raised them, too. She raised all of them. She raised her children, her grandchildren, and one of her great-grandchildren. She cared for them and raised them. I don't know how she did it.

Her husband, my grandfather Joe, was still living, but he had gone blind in the early 1930s due to cataracts. Back in those days, you couldn't get an operation on cataracts. So he went completely blind. She had to care for him, too, as a matter of fact. But my mother's youngest brother was still at home. He didn't marry until late in life. So he was there, and he did all the farming and all that. Later on, he did marry and had several children, and they lived there with my grandmother, too! She had a hand in raising those children also. She was quite a woman. When I would go to visit her at the farm, I would visit all my cousins also. I enjoyed visiting with her because we had lots to eat and lots of companions to play with.

Esther, my mother, was one of the six children born to Joe and Mary, three girls and three boys. The oldest girl, as I mentioned earlier, died before I was born. One boy died in early childhood when he accidentally drank lye water when Grandma Shuman was washing clothes. The oldest sister was named Gertrude (Trudy), and the brother who died accidentally as a child was named Ledford. All members of the Shuman family who died before about 1940 are buried in the Little Creek Church cemetery located off the Clyde road, now in the middle of the Camp Stewart Military Reservation. The others, besides my mother and the two previously mentioned, were Robert (Uncle Bobby), Juanita (Aunt Nita), and the youngest, Earl. I do not recall other details except they lived on my grandma Shuman's farm. They lived for many years up the road in a one-room log cabin we called "The Old House." Some years later, they were able to build "The New House" up on the main road between Lanier and the Clyde Highway. My grandpa Shuman was a member of the second generation of the Shumans who came to the area from Dresden, Germany. He had claimed a grant of land in Georgia. The date he settled is unknown, but I guess it must have been in the mid 1800s. Many tales were told of the extremely hard times he and his family had making it because it was nothing like he expected and the location on the Canoochee was jungle-like with poor, sandy soil. I don't remember the date of Grandpa Shuman's birth, but he was one of twins. The other twin died in an accident before I was born. I only recall one of his brothers, Uncle Hamp Shuman, who lived near where the other Shumans settled. The original spelling of the surname was Schuman, but sometime over the years, the *c* was dropped and the spelling became "Shuman."

My grandmother, Mary Downs Shuman, was one of six children. Great-grandfather Downs was a landowner with extensive property, and when he died, each child received enough land to make a nice farm. Uncle Billie received that portion which included the original homestead.

CHAPTER 3

The Early
Futches

I do not know any of the Futch family history prior to my grandfather, John O. Futch, but apparently this branch of the Futch family had been in the Bulloch County area for some time. We do know the original Futches came to the British colonies before the American Revolution and settled in New Jersey. There were two Futch brothers who came together to the colonies. Therefore, there are two related branches of the family. Descendants of the original Futch brothers migrated south and then west. This was a common migration route at that time. Some of these descendants settled in North Carolina, South Carolina, and Georgia, and later west to Mississippi, Louisiana, and Texas. Some of these descendants settled in the Bulloch County area.

John Owen Futch was born on February 5, 1843, in Bulloch County, Georgia. He joined the Georgia forces of the Confederate Army sometime in the early 1860s. When he joined, he was accompanied by his young uncle, who was approximately his same age. He and his young uncle were sent to join the Confederate forces in north Georgia commanded by General Joseph Johnston. We know he served throughout the campaign and both he and his uncle—I do not know the uncle's name—were at the Battle of Kennesaw Mountain, and we know both served with the artillery. My father told me that his father recounted many times how difficult it was to pull the cannon up the side of Kennesaw with horses. He told of being present when his young uncle was killed. Before he died, his uncle asked him to please try to get back home to Bulloch County so he could tell the family what happened.

After Atlanta fell, my grandfather Futch continued to serve under General Hood, who had assumed command from General Johnston, who had been relieved by the Confederate President Davis. He was with the remains of General Hood's army in Tennessee when the war ended. He told of having to walk to south Georgia from Tennessee since no transportation was available. He became a farmer and carpenter. He married Elizabeth Woodcock, and they had eighteen children. Little is known about the Woodcock family. Grover Cleveland, my father, was the seventeenth of these eighteen. John and his wife are buried in the Red Hill Primitive Baptist Church graveyard. He helped to build the church building, which still stands today.

All of the John O. Futch descendants remained in the southeast Georgia area except brothers James and John, who moved to the Orlando, Florida, area sometime in the mid to late 1920s. I remember seeing these two uncles only once, in the early 1930s when Grandmother Futch (Elizabeth Woodcock Futch) died and they came back to Georgia for the funeral. After that, we lost contact with these relatives. So, today there are cousins and other relatives in the Orlando, Florida, area that we do not know.

My father, Grover C. Futch, was born on February 12, 1893, in Bulloch County, Georgia. When World War I came, he was at an age that he could serve. He told me he volunteered for service, but they would not take him because he was married with small children. Sometime about 1909–11, Grover C., known as Cleveland by all his brothers and sisters, met and began dating Frances Esther Shuman.

Cleveland and Esther were married in 1912. Their first child was born in 1913. In all, they had eight children. Joseph Alva was born October 12, 1913; Verna was born October 24, 1915; Esther Odell was born October 14, 1918; Cecil Lee was born September 12, 1920; Latrell was born August 10, 1922; Grover C., Jr., was born September 16, 1924; Mary Elizabeth was born September 15, 1926; and Gloria Ernestine was born December 9, 1929. Gloria Ernestine died as an infant on December 20, 1929. She was buried in the Little Creek Cemetery.

CHAPTER 4

The Futch Siblings

Joseph Alva Futch was the first child of Cleveland and Esther Futch and was born October 20, 1913. He was known as Alva by the family. He married Eloise Conner when we lived on what we called the Aunt Ag place in Bulloch County. He could possibly have been called for duty during World War II, but was not because of being married with several small children. Alva learned to operate construction equipment and did this work most of his life. He and Eloise lived in or near Pembroke until after World War II, when he moved his family to Florida in the vicinity of Orlando. He continued to live in this area until sometime in the mid-60s, when he and Eloise were divorced.

He returned to Bryan County after the divorce and for a while had two children with him, James and Junior. After returning to Georgia, he married two other times and lived in the small community of Daisy, between Pembroke and Claxton. As far as I can recall, he and Eloise had eight children who remained in Florida, most in the Orlando area. They are Harry, Betty, Elizabeth, Daniel, Brenda, Billy James and Junior. Alva died after a short illness in 1978, as I recall. He is buried in the Pembroke Cemetery in the Futch lot.

Verna Futch Pevey was the second child of Cleveland and Esther. She was born October 24, 1915. I have many fond memories of her as an older sister. She was able to drive the car in 1929. I remember her looking after the rest of us when Gloria Ernestine was born and died. She met and married Sam Pevey in 1933. As I recall, it was Grandma Shuman who had introduced them. After they were married, Sam tried his hand at tobacco farming in Bulloch County. After that, for several years he operated stores on the Savannah-Statesboro Highway, not too far from Blitchton near Pembroke (the same place my father operated in 1941 and '42). After that they moved to Savannah, where Sam worked for a bakery for several years and then finally went to work for Sears Roebuck & Company as an appliance salesman, where he remained until he retired. They had three children: Caroline, Janet, and Sam, Jr. They bought a home on Delta Circle, Savannah, where they remained until both died.

Esther Odell Futch Walters was born October 14, 1918, the third child of Cleveland and Esther. The one thing I remember about Odell, as told to me, was her bout with blood poisoning in her leg when she was only four or five years old. She almost lost the leg, but at the time we were living in Savannah, where much better care was available, and they were able to save her life and her leg. It was caused by a nail she had somehow stuck in her leg. I recall a picture my mother had of her and the nurses at the hospital when she was learning to walk again. All through her life she has carried two scars from this illness, which almost cost her life. Sometime in the mid to late 1930s, she met and married a young man by the name of Glisson. This marriage lasted only a short time. They were divorced. Later we learned he was in the Philippine Islands when World War II broke out, and he died in the infamous Japanese death march.

Sometime later, she married W. D. Smutty Crumpton from the Claxton area. They had one son, Robert (Bobbie). Odell and Smutty lived most of the time in Savannah and lived for a brief period in Dania, Florida, just north of Miami. She and Smutty were divorced in the late '40s or early '50s, and then she married Bill Walters. They had one son, Michael, born in July 1958. After a few years, Bill died and Odell continued to live in Savannah. After our father died, she helped our mother out on weekends, and eventually she and Mike moved to Pembroke. She continued to live there until our mother and Cecil died. She then moved to Statesboro because of failing health and to be near Bobby, who lived there. She had a small apartment in Statesboro, and was a semi-invalid because of severe back problems for which she had several operations.

Cecil Lee Futch was born September 12, 1920, the fourth child of Cleveland and Esther. At the beginning of World War II, he and Marilyn Hall had a son, Robert. There has always been some question as to whether they were married, but I can only assume they were. He was called into service during World War II in 1942. After basic training, he was assigned to the Medical Corps and served overseas in India with a general hospital unit. When the Korean War began in the early 1950s, he again entered the Army and served for several months. He was not sent overseas during this tour of duty. After World War II, he remained in Pembroke, working at various jobs until he went back in service during the Korean Conflict. After this, he returned to Pembroke. He worked at various jobs, working for our cousin Jack Shuman in the building supply business, but most of his work was with the state highway department.

Some years later, he married again and lived in a mobile home across the road from our mother. This marriage did not work because of his drinking. He continued after this to live with our mother until she died in 1982 and her place was sold. He then moved into an apartment near Odell and continued to live there until he died. To me there were two great tragedies in his life. The first is the fact that he drank excessively and went on frequent binges. At times he would remain intoxicated for up to three or four weeks, and these episodes would come about every three or four months, more or less. Because of this drinking problem, he could not hold a job for very long, nor could he maintain any kind of married life. The second, and I think both went together, was the fact that he was illiterate. He was ashamed of this and hid it always. My mother said often he would not go to school, nor could they make him, and when he did go, he would make no attempt to learn anything. Finally, in part because they moved around so much during the 1930's, they gave up, and he grew up without a basic formal education, knowing only how to write his name.

Latrell Futch Ledford was born on August 10, 1922, the fifth child of Cleveland and Esther. In perhaps 1938 or '39, Latrell married Barney Burnsed, whom she had met when our father ran a store on the old Savannah-Statesboro Highway at a place called Five Mile Bend. The Burnsed family lived just up the road. The whole Burnsed family of father and four boys did automobile bodywork. They lived most of their married years in the Savannah area except for a time in Florida and Pembroke. They had two daughters, Fay and Gail. Barney had always been a heavy drinker and finally became a complete alcoholic. Because of this and the fact he could not hold a job, he and Latrell divorced. She later met and married David Ledford, who was a career man in the Air Force, stationed at Hunter Field in Savannah. They had two sons, Donald and Arthur. They were transferred several times before David retired, including Puerto Rico and Midway. David finally retired, and they lived in Haysville, North Carolina, which was David's original home.

Grover Cleveland Futch, Jr., was born on September 16, 1924, the sixth child of Cleveland and Esther.

Mary Elizabeth was born on September 16, 1926, the seventh child of Cleveland and Esther. She married Hannie Burnsed, Barney's brother, about 1942. They had four boys: Freddie, Buddy, and twins Johnny and Joey. Hannie was also an automotive body and fender craftsman and most of their time was spent in the area of Pembroke and Savannah. The oldest son, Freddie, is deceased and buried in the Futch lot at Northside Cemetery in Pembroke. Hannie is deceased, but before his death he and Mary were divorced. She still resides in Pembroke today.

Gloria Ernestine Futch was born on December 9, 1929, the eighth child of Cleveland and Esther. She died on December 20, 1929. She is buried in the Little Creek Cemetery.

The Ford Motor Company introduced this logo in 1928,
the year G.C. Futch, Sr., was able to buy a new Ford.

CHAPTER 5

Hard Times

When the crash of 1929 came, my father, Cleveland, lost his job with the transit company because everybody was laying people off. There were no jobs. He decided to move the family back to the country. So we moved back to Pembroke, and he went to work for the Warnell family, probably the biggest landowners in the county. The Warnells had hundreds of acres in naval stores, which is the turpentine business. My father's job was to supervise crews of black workers working in the woods. The Warnell family provided a house for us to live in, located on their property near the turpentine still, the quarters for the black workers, and the commissary in Pembroke. But before we moved into the house, we lived briefly in a small four-room house near the railroad tracks in town. I still remember being awakened by the trains coming through at night, although I was only about five years old.

It was while we were living in the Warnell house that Gloria Ernestine was born and died. Although I was just five, I remember it as distinctly as if it were just yesterday. I remember my mother's grief and how she was unable to go to the cemetery because she was recovering from the birth and how the weather was extremely cold for that time of year. Gloria, too, is buried in the Little Creek Cemetery.

The following year, 1930 or '31, we moved to a farmhouse in the lower part of Bulloch on the Pembroke-Statesboro Road. My father later decided that he wanted to get back to farming, even though by that time times were awfully hard. So, we moved, and he leased a farm up in the edge of Bulloch County—up where Georgia Southern is—and he was going to farm. This was the place we knew as the Aunt Ag place.

It was while we lived here that Alva met and married his wife, Eloise Connor. It was also when we lived here that I got to know some of my cousins from the Futch side of the family, some of my father's sisters, Aunt Sula's children, and Dan Futch, Uncle Tink's son. They lived a couple of miles nearby. There was also

Aunt Esther and her children, who also lived only a couple of miles away. But the first year he farmed it rained all summer long. There were no crops. He had a tremendous field of cotton, but only made a half bale. By that time, the Depression was really rough. At that point he planned to move, but we were able to get some government food for a time.

We later moved back near to Pembroke, in 1932, to a house just north of town called the Emory Smith place. This was located on the road from Pembroke to the Ashes Branch Community. I don't recall what my father did for a livelihood during this time, but I think it was still turpentine work. During the summer, we always had a big garden to help out. It was while we were living here that Verna met and married Sam. They were married December 23, 1933. We were there perhaps a year and a half or two years. From there we moved again. Over the next several years we moved a total of sixteen times! If we had had a family farm where we could live and have our own food, it would have been better, but my father had no work, so we moved from place to place.

In the early part of 1934, we again moved to a farm, which we called the old Cox place, located not far from Grandma Shuman. It was on the same road, but back toward the community of Lanier. I don't recall much about the place or how long we were there. The Great Depression was in full effect. There were no jobs to be had. To help out, many people at that time dabbled in making illegal whiskey or moonshine. We were no exception, but it did not go on for very long and to any great degree. We later moved to the little town of Blitchton, where my father went to work again for the Warnell family; they had quite a large turpentine operation nearby. This arrangement lasted several months until the Warnells accused my father of stealing a pistol from their commissary. He always believed it was one of the Warnells that had stolen it, but that didn't matter. He left them and we moved to Savannah for a short time.

It was while we were living in Blitchton that the "chicken incident" happened. Some of my nieces like to hear me tell this story. From the time we lived at the Aunt Ag place, my mother moved her chickens with us each time we moved. She kept her chickens for eggs to help in her cooking. We moved the chickens at night after they had gone to roost. There were still five of us children at home, Odell being the oldest. One day our parents were gone for the entire day and we had very little to eat. So we came up with the idea to catch and fry one of my mother's chickens for lunch. We caught the chicken and my sister Odell did the butchering and cooking. It was indeed a wonderful lunch! We all agreed to keep what we had done a secret and not tell my mother. I was the one who "let the cat out of the bag" later by something I said, so I had to tell her the whole story. Needless to say, she was not too upset. Shortly thereafter, she got rid of the chickens since we were moving into Savannah after a short stay in the small community of Monteith.

In 1928, my father was able to buy a new Ford car, which was a touring-type car, so he cut it down and made a little pickup out of it. I was four years old. I can remember seeing my reflection in the shiny new doors. I also remember the first time it rained and we couldn't find the curtains to put up. We had to go back to J. C. Lewis, where he had bought the car, and they showed him where they were stored, in a compartment underneath the floor mats in front of the back seat.

While we were in Savannah, he ran a little wood yard, selling mostly kindling that you'd use to start fires with, because everybody had a little fireplace—there was no central heat then—and he sold the kindling to little neighborhood grocery stores. There weren't any supermarkets or anything like that.

The next several years, 1934 to 1937 or '38, we moved a total of eight times. First, near a small community called Monteith, near Savannah, then into Savannah itself on Gordon Street. In each place, it was only for a few months, or even weeks, in some instances. Next we moved back to Pembroke and stayed with

Alva and Eloise for a very short period of time, then to a place about three miles outside of Pembroke on the Clyde Road, which we called the Duggar place. We next moved down to the Downs Town community to a fairly decent house, but the owners forced us to move after just a few weeks to a shack just down the road. We were there a short time and then moved to a real shack belonging to Perry Parish, located on the Clyde Highway. It was 1936.

It was here things reached as low a point as I remember during the Depression of the '30s. All during this time, my father managed to keep body and soul together by selling kindling wood. That was the real low point—that was probably the low point prior to World War II. I can remember at times we had nothing to eat. I remember specifically that my father went to Mr. Parish on one occasion and Mr. Parish gave him a bag of meal, some flour, some eggs, and several ham bones where the main part of the ham had already been used. That spring, Mr. Parish also gave us a plot of land in the corner of one of his nearby fields to use for a garden. That summer also the blackberry crop was good and we had plenty of berries to help out, too. I remember going to school that year with one pair of overalls. I wore them each day, and my mother would wash them each afternoon.

My father's old truck had broken down and was parked under a tree. We had no money for parts to repair it. My sister Latrell—two years older than I—and I had malaria fever. While we were sick, we saw no doctor. We were out of our heads with high temperatures, but we did not see a doctor. I can remember I felt like I was floating in the air. I was out of my head. I can remember coming back to sanity once in a while during this fever and my head was hurting so badly I thought it would burst. They found my sister Latrell wandering out through the woods one day. She didn't know where she was.

G. C. Futch, Jr., with his guitar, 1938

CHAPTER 6

Prospects Brighten

Fortunately, we both survived. Our family moved back into Pembroke. That was at the end of about 1937. By that time, things were beginning to look a little bit better. My father went to work on the WPA for a while, which provided us with money to buy food. That was a federal government program: the Works Progress Administration. In high school, there was a youth administration program, something similar to the WPA. High school students could work around the school, cleaning up, trimming shrubbery, and things like that. I got a little check from the government every so often, and I just would turn that over to my family to buy groceries.

Somehow my father managed to get parts for the car and finally got it fixed. While we were there on the Parish place, I got my first guitar. My cousin, Bernice Shuman, had bought a guitar and wanted to sell it, and my sister Odell helped me buy it. As I recall, it was only $7.00. I had a small amount of money I had earned along with my brother Cecil by accumulating about a half barrel of pine tar and selling it.

It was during the winter of 1936, probably early December or late November, that we moved to Pembroke again to a house across the street from my brother Alva where we had stayed for a short time at one point in the past. We were there until 1937, when we moved around the corner into a little house by a railroad track that we had lived in briefly in 1929. As I recall, we were here until late 1941 or early 1942, not long after Pearl Harbor. We were living there when Latrell married her first husband, Barney Burnsed.

From there we moved to a place west of Pembroke on the Claxton Highway. This was a beer and wine shop my father was going to operate, and we lived upstairs. My brother-in-law, Sam Pevey, had run the same place earlier. This didn't last too long and we moved to a small white rental house in Pembroke on a street in front of the water tank and community house.

By that time, we were beginning to prepare for World War II. The government was buying up land to make an aircraft training center in Bryan County, in that area. So they bought up all this land and cut the county in two. My father got work finally, first with a contractor building bridges and other improvements in the Camp Stewart area and then with the shipyards in Savannah.

The Depression was finally over for good, it seemed. My father was later able to save enough money to buy a 40-acre farm just north of Pembroke on the Statesboro Highway known as the Hall place. I recall he bought it from Dr. M. K. Smith, one of the doctors in Pembroke. We lived in the house near the water tank until perhaps 1946 or 1947, when he fixed up the old place on the Hall place and we moved out there.

Things were looking better, and I was able to attend high school. (I was the only one in my family to finish high school and the only one to get a college degree.) We lived there in Pembroke until I graduated from high school in 1943. I was supposed to have graduated in 1942, but I missed a year when I was so sick. I graduated in 1943 and was valedictorian of my class. When Pearl Harbor came, I was already seventeen years old, so I knew I would soon be going in the service. They were already drafting, and they were talking about drafting down to eighteen. So I had to register with the draft as soon as I was eighteen.

G. C. Futch, Jr., in 1943

CHAPTER 7

Preparing for War

I graduated from high school at eighteen. I had to get a deferment to finish high school, but as soon as I finished high school, I was called right in to service. I graduated in May 1943, and within days was ordered to report for duty by the local draft board. At that time, there were so many people volunteering for certain branches—Air Corps, Navy—that all voluntary enlistments were stopped for a period of about two years. So they were drafting at that time for all branches of service. I went into the infantry. I reported to Fort McPherson in Atlanta in late May 1943, and after a few days of processing, was sent by train to Camp Wheeler near Macon, Georgia.

The training at Camp Wheeler was rough as it was in the middle of summer, the temperature sometimes reaching over 100 degrees. It was an unusually hot summer, even for Middle Georgia. It was certainly the hottest summer I'd ever experienced in my life. Most of the time it was so hot during the day that we were not able to be outside training, and they would give us a half a day off. We would train at night. We'd take a twenty mile hike. We'd go out ten miles, pitch tents for a short time, then get some rest. Then we'd march back. I lost approximately thirty pounds, going from about 185 to 155.

I was assigned to the 6th Training Battalion for basic training and company-clerk school because I could type and take shorthand. I had typing and shorthand in high school, and this was a special battalion with a school for training company clerks. Company clerks keep the records in an infantry company, daily reports and other records. In that particular battalion, in addition to company clerks, there was one company where they'd train cooks and bakers. In another, they trained buglers. The buglers trained in the woods where we couldn't hear them. The last company was truck drivers and engineers. So my battalion was a specialized battalion.

After basic training, I was given a delay in route, and I went home for about ten days. Then we had orders to report to Fort

Mead, Maryland. My best friend in high school was named Eddie Bacon. We went into service together. We went to training together, we served together, and we came home together, and we both reported to Fort Mead at the same time. So, Eddie and I caught the train to Fort Mead, in Maryland, and we were there for several weeks being reclassified—more physicals—and then we were sent to a little camp in Massachusetts called Camp Miles Standish. It was a POE (Port of Embarkation) camp for the Port of Boston, so I knew we were on the way overseas, but we were not told where or when.

I was there with my friend Eddie for Christmas of 1943. By now, the weather was extremely cold and the temporary barracks we were housed in were heated by two coal-burning heaters, but the bathrooms were outside in a separate building. This was one of the few times while in service I wore long underwear, both top and bottom. While we were there, we did some training and some marching, but most of the time we were left to ourselves. And most of that time was spent in the PX where the jukebox was going all the time. The two main tunes I remember were "Paper Doll" by the Mills Brothers and "White Christmas" by Bing Crosby. They played over and over and over on the jukebox. So today, if I hear "Paper Doll," I automatically associate it with Camp Miles Standish. We remained there through Christmas of 1943, and we were told to get ready to leave the day after Christmas. We did not know where we were going, but we assumed either England or the Mediterranean. Within a couple of days, we were boarding a ship, the S. S. *Alexander*, in Boston Harbor and left and joined another group of ships out of New York. It was a tremendous convoy. The troop ships were in the middle and on the outside there were an aircraft carrier, cruisers, and destroyers going up and down to try to keep the German U-boats away from the troop ships. It was a tremendous convoy.

CHAPTER 8

Buzz Bombs
over London

It took about eight days to cross the Atlantic, and we landed in Liverpool in early January of 1944. It was probably mid-afternoon when we disembarked and went directly to the train. We left Liverpool and went to south England to a little town called Yeoville, where a replacement depot was located. We remained there for probably about two weeks. There was a tremendous bulletin board outside. You had to watch that bulletin board every day to see if you were posted to leave. Well, after about two weeks, there was a list posted of twenty names, and my name was on that list, and so was my friend Eddie's name, and also the names of some others that we knew from

Camp Wheeler.

We found out that we were going to London, England. The headquarters we were sent to in London was called FUSAG (First U. S. Army Group). We got on the train and went to London and disembarked and caught the tube—the subway—and rode to Marble Arch Station. We found out that we would be part of General Omar Bradley's new group headquarters. At that time, he had a dual command: Commanding General 1st Army and Commanding General 1st U. S. Army Group. Group headquarters was responsible for planning details of the invasion of mainland Europe with the British. General Eisenhower decided general plans, and FUSAG and the British worked out the details. Our job was to coordinate plans with the British for the invasion that was coming. I was assigned to a G1, which is the personnel section, to an office called Special Service. That particular office was responsible for entertainment of the troops. A colonel was in charge of that office, and his job was to coordinate entertainment for the troops once they got ashore. I did the typing and kept the records. But toward the end—I guess it was sometime in May of 1944—I was assigned to go on detached service to the British 21st Army Group commanded by General Montgomery, across town from where we were in London. I knew the invasion was imminent, but I didn't know the date. I had top secret clearance and knew a lot of information, but we didn't talk anything about it at all. When the invasion came, I was still on detached service with the British.

Right after the invasion, probably the first or second night, is when the Germans started sending over the V-1 Buzz Bombs over London. A buzz bomb was a flying bomb. It made a peculiar noise and once it cut off, it came down. So if you saw one coming down, you'd better hide, get somewhere, otherwise it would just go on past.

That winter when we first came to London, the Germans had renewed their blitz against the city. Almost every night there were air raids over London, but we got used to it. Most of the time they came in the middle of the night, and we just went down to another lower floor from where we were billeted. But one night our billet was hit by incendiaries. So was our headquarters with all of our top secret papers. While we were trying to put the fire out in our building, we were called out to go over to the headquarters and guard the top secret material, and put out the fire over there. While I was gone, somebody decided that our building would burn and all personnel and personal belongings were thrown outside. So I lost all my personal stuff. It all had to be reissued.

At the same time, a 500-pound German bomb hit right in

front of our building, but it was a dud! It went down under the cement into the ground, and the British had to get it out days later. It turned out that a lot of the incendiaries were duds. I was on about the third floor and one came through the window and landed on my bed, but didn't go off at the time. I was down below on another floor. I kept it for some time as a souvenir. But it was a live bomb, and I later decided I should get rid of it, so we disposed of it.

When we had the attack on our billet, we had two men wounded in that raid and they received Purple Hearts. We had one incendiary bomb come through the roof, through the wall, and it wounded one man standing against the wall. It hit him in the back. The other one was injured while he was further down in the building. It was kind of unusual to receive a Purple Heart while in London, but it so happened they both were injured by German bombs, so their injuries qualified them for the award.

After the buzz bombs started after the invasion, from the first night they came over, we always ran outside to see the fireworks, with the search lights and the German planes. You could see them sometimes. The first one that came over—it came right over the top of the building, with the flame coming out of the end of it—we thought was a plane on fire that had just been hit, but it was a buzz bomb. When I was going back and forth to the 21st Army Group, we could see them all during the day. They were coming from Holland, across the Channel, aimed at London. I lost a lot of sleep. So when they asked for volunteers to move to headquarters in France, I was an eager volunteer. I was in the first group, which was a small group of about 100 enlisted men with several officers.

FRANCE

CHAPTER 9

Omaha
Beach

We caught the train down to a staging area near South Hampton for shipment to Normandy. We arrived there a short time later. After a few days' delay due to bad weather, we boarded a troop ship to go to cross the Channel. When I arrived, it was—I've forgotten the exact time—probably "D" plus two weeks to three weeks. We did not have a port yet, so everything had to come in on the beach. So I landed on Omaha Beach on, probably, "D" plus 21 days after the initial invasion. We had to climb overboard, get down into landing craft, and land on the beach.

The beach area was a beehive of activity because everything

had to come in on the beaches. We landed and went off Omaha Beach, up the slope up to the top of the surrounding hill. We set up camp in an apple orchard back from the beach about two miles. At this time, the front was three to four miles inland, and we could hear artillery in the distance. While we were going up from the beach, up the hill, to our left was a draw. On the other side of that is where the present cemetery is located on Omaha Beach.

They had just started the cemetery. They had probably two or three dozen white crosses or Stars of David already up. What shook us up was the sight of all the bodies laid out to be buried. There were so many. I had never seen or even imagined such a sight. It is still difficult to remember that scene.

* * * * *

We set up camp about three miles back in the apple orchard. We were there, oh, probably about a month. While there, we experienced our first and only gas alert. It came in the middle of the night, but proved to be false. A sentry on guard had mistaken the smell of some gun powder for gas and had given the alarm. After perhaps an hour of wearing gas masks, a public address system truck from Civilian Affairs rode up and down the front giving the "all clear" over loudspeakers.

We had almost complete air dominance. The exception was that the Germans were still able to get a few planes up at night. At night we had raids all along the beach. Because we were just inland a little bit, we didn't get any direct hits on us, but they were always dropping bombs and strafing the beach area. But the main thing, though, was the anti-aircraft shells. They exploded and made a lot of shrapnel, and the shrapnel would come raining down on us through the trees. A lot of the fellows would just get up against a tree when this happened. I dug myself a deep foxhole and when this happened, I'd just jump in it!

For a while, we had one unwelcome visitor in the middle of every afternoon, one German pilot who would fly down the beach. I guess he was reconnoitering. Finally, one afternoon they were able to get him. He bailed out, but did not escape. He was captured right down in front of where we were.

We were there until the breakout through the German line at Saint Lô was completed. After the breakout at Saint Lô, we moved the field headquarters twice.

The first time we moved was near a town called Coutanches We—the enlisted personnel—were still living in pup tents. This was at a big French chateau. We had our offices inside that building, but we all lived outside in tents. One afternoon, while we were all in our tent area, a young man whose tent was near ours committed suicide. He shot himself in the chest. He couldn't take the pressure of not knowing where we were going. We were not in any particular danger, but we could have been. After we heard the shot, we went up to where the sound had come from and found that he had shot himself. They got him to a field hospital, but he died shortly thereafter. That was the only person I ever saw that didn't want to go and fulfill his duty.

Each time we moved, we could see the destruction: dead dairy cattle killed by artillery, burned-out tanks, disabled trucks, and other debris. Occasionally, we spotted a dead German soldier who had not yet been buried.

CHAPTER 10

The European Theater

By about the first of August, we had enough units ashore that the 3rd Army was broken off and given to General Patton. The 1st Army command went to General Hodges. General Bradley became the group commander. He had been group commander all the time, but we became officially operational as the 12th Army Group on August the 1st, 1944. He commanded the 1st and 3rd Armies and then later on the 9th Army was added under General Simpson. He commanded the three armies all the way through to the end of the war in Europe. After Coutanches, our next move was to Versailles, right outside of Paris. Our camp was right across the street from the Palace of

Versailles. While I was there, we got to tour the palace grounds and the inside of the palace. During our stay in Versailles, the U. S. O. had a show on the grounds at the palace and, as I recall, the main acts were Fred Astaire and Dinah Shore. I got to go in to Paris one afternoon with two buddies and we got to see quite a few things, and we went to the Folies Bergères. It was a girlie show, but it was very refined and very spectacular. It was quite a nice show.

From Versailles, the armies moved quite further east. Our next move (always keeping just back of the front), was to a town called Verdun. It was in this area and in the nearby town of Metz where so much of the trench warfare of World War I happened. We occupied an abandoned French Army garrison which had also been used by the retreating Germans. While there, I got to visit all the old World War I areas. I was working all this time, too, though we did have a lot of time on our own.

There was one particular area where an artillery shell had hit almost on top of a trench in World War I. It caved in on all of the French soldiers in that area. What they did was they left a section of this trench as it was and all you could see was the top of their bayonets, about a foot of the bayonet, sticking up out of the dirt. They left it there as a memorial. It was all covered with a marble building. I thought that was quite something that they would leave this. It was as if they had their rifles at the ready.

We were in Verdun quite a long time, about nine months, because the winter had come, and the fighting had stalled. I spent Christmas 1944 there. While we were there, the Germans still did a little bombing and strafing, and also while we were there the Battle of the Bulge started, on December 19, 1944. Our advance echelon was up in Luxembourg City. They were very close to where the Germans broke through in the Ardennes Forest, which was the start of the famous battle. Verdun was located just south and slightly east of the battle. During this time, we were on full alert to pull out, and most of us had to take new physical exams in case we were needed for replacements in the infantry.

It was also while we were in Verdun that for the first time Women Army Corps personnel, WACs, came to work in the headquarters. They worked in many offices in the group headquarters. My office was one of the smallest, consisting of one officer from Rising Sun, Indiana, two enlisted men, and me. (By this time I was a sergeant.)

My good friend Eugene Basset, from Minnesota, and I were in charge of arranging field entertainment for the troops. During my time there, we arranged shows by Bing Crosby, Mickey Rooney—I met him and we spent perhaps three to four hours together in the office—and Marlene Dietrich.

The Battle of the Bulge held us up for quite a while. It was quite a time for us because there was a lot of uncertainty connected with the breakthrough of the German Army. But finally it was straightened out and the German Army really was defeated, so we went on into Germany. The next move for our award-winning detachment—we won a meritorious unit award—was to Wiesbaden, Germany.

The Army had a "no fraternization" policy, but we all had quite plush offices in Wiesbaden, taken over from the Germans. It was while we were in Wiesbaden that we got the news of the first atomic bomb being dropped on Japan. The news came over an Armed Forces Radio announcement. There was no official announcement by the U. S. Army. There was one universal sigh of relief because this meant the war in the Pacific would end soon. Many of us had wondered when we would be sent to the Pacific Theater and feared it would be soon. Some advance units had already been sent to the Pacific.

The fighting ended and by August the 1st the war was over in Europe, so the 12th Army Group was disbanded as there was no longer the need for a combat group headquarters in the field. Before General Bradley left, he had each person come into his office, and he shook hands with each one of us and told us how much he appreciated our service. So I got to meet him on that occasion. I had seen him many times, but not to speak to him. I had seen General Eisenhower and General Patton. I'd seen them up close, but didn't get to meet them, of course. I saw General Eisenhower in London, and also in Verdun when the Battle of the Bulge started. They all came in to Verdun for a strategy meeting: General Simpson, General Patton, and, of course, General Eisenhower. It gave me the opportunity to see some of the history of World War II being made.

G. C. Futch, Jr., at age twenty in Wiesbaden, Germany, in 1945, the 12th U. S. Army Group.

CHAPTER 11

The Machine Records Unit

After the 12th Army Group was deactivated, I was transferred to Frankfurt, Germany. And there I worked in ETOUSA Headquarters. (ETOUSA stands for European Theater of Operations U. S. Army.) It was commanded by General Eisenhower, who, in addition to being the Supreme Allied Commander, was also commander of all American troops in Europe. So this headquarters is the one that dealt only with American troops in Europe. The other was a tactical headquarters that dealt with the war itself.

When I went to Frankfurt, I was put in a division called Machine Records Unit. We worked with equipment that was the forerunner of computers. It was all IBM equipment, much of which was captured from the Germans. IBM had maintained quite extensive operations in Germany before the war.

I was in charge of the keypunch section. We punched data cards; we were keeping records of mostly Nazi party members and war criminals and other personnel files. I did that until early December of 1945. I'd been in Europe two years.

I never worried too much about serving because I saw it as something that had to be done, and did it because my loyalty was never in question. But over the years with things in our country going like they have, I deem it more and more a privilege to have served. I was never mindful of my danger, but took it one day at a time since I knew the Army would do everything it could to get me home safely.

CHAPTER 12

Homecoming

In December 1945, I got orders to come home. There was a small group of us. The order in which you got to come home was based on a point system. You got points for the number of months you'd been overseas, the number of awards you got, and a lot of things like that. Well, of course I'd been overseas for almost two years, and I had received five Battle Stars, and there was so much for each one. I had received the Invasion of Normandy, Northern France, Battle of the Bulge, Rhineland —I'd crossed the Rhine—and then Central Europe. The reason I mention that is because that helped me get home. There were so many points for each one.

We boarded the train in Frankfurt, and I was due to go back to Le Havre, France, and leave from there. Well, we got back as far as Paris and there weren't enough ships coming to take us all home. So, a group of us was taken off and stationed in Paris for a while. We were housed in a building called the Petite Palace, just one block off the main street in Paris, right off the Champs Elysées, just almost at the site of the Arc de Triomphe, and of course the Eiffel Tower is right there, too. Notre Dame was just across the river. I worked in the Comzone—Command Zone—Headquarters. That's where I was assigned, but I really didn't do anything. I just went to an office every day and just sat! I was there probably about two weeks. It gave me the opportunity to see Paris, which I had not had when in nearby Versailles.

But, finally, they called us back. We got on the train again and went to Le Havre to the port of embarkation camp called Camp Lucky Strike. They were all named for cigarettes. I was just there a few days when we boarded the troop ship USS *Le Jeune* to come home. It was a single Navy ship, and we crossed the Atlantic again in about seven or eight days. We got in a bad storm coming back, and everybody was sick. Even I got a little seasick, and that was very unusual for me.

We finally got to New York and sailed into the harbor where they had waterspouts going from the tugboats. (This was done to welcome each troop ship back home.) The Statue of Liberty was over there on the left. We disembarked from the boat and got the train, and went to Camp Kilmer, New Jersey. We were there for a short time and caught the train again. We went by train everywhere.

We caught another train to Camp Gordon, Georgia, outside of Augusta, and I was discharged on December 12, 1945.

While I was at Camp Gordon, I ran into my old friend Eddie again. We had been separated for the first time when we moved from the beach area in Normandy. General Bradley had realized that the headquarters had grown to such size it was cumbersome to move all at one time, so he created a smaller group. Our code name was Eagle Main, and he created a small group with just a few people from each department that he could move ahead faster. It was called Eagle Tac. Eddie was in that group and I stayed with Eagle Main. So, after the war, we saw each other briefly in Wiesbaden, and then I went to Frankfurt and he went somewhere else. And here we were, together again. He had gotten to the Camp Gordon separation center just a few days before I did. He got home just a few days before I arrived in Pembroke.

And that was the end of my Army service. "My adventure," I called it.

But I was lucky. I went over as an infantry replacement and most of the men that I was with in the replacement depot—I mentioned that about twenty of us were called out to go to London—they went to Omaha Beach on D-Day. I could have been in that group. Then later on, when the Battle of the Bulge came about, infantry replacements became scarce. When a man was killed, he had to be replaced. So they would go through all the headquarters searching for people who had infantry basic. And I had, of course, at Camp Wheeler, so I had to take a physical and be ready to go to the front, to be assigned to a front-line division. But, fortunately, about the time I was ready to go, they began to get a lot of replacements in from the States. They got a lot of men from the Air Force and from other places. So I didn't have to go up to the front then.

But back to my story. After I got home, I had nothing. I had no definite plans. I didn't know what to do.

The author in civilian clothes in 1945

G. C. and Mildred on their wedding day, June 1, 1950. Nashville, Tennessee

CHAPTER 13

The G.I. Bill, Mildred, and Me

My parents were still in the small house near the water tank when I returned from the service. I was 20 years old. The post-war settlement had come in. It was kind of a recession at that time, so I just stayed around for almost a year and finally I decided to go to a teacher's college, Georgia Southern—it was Georgia Teacher's College at that time—and enrolled in the fall of 1946. Off I went, and I never lived in Pembroke again. It wasn't so much that I wanted to be a teacher, it's just that that was the closest college. So, Eddie and I, we enrolled at the same time and went together there. We both got a degree from there. He went into teaching; I did not. They had about 350 students when I first went there, but when I left they had, oh, I guess around 500. I was in the first group of servicemen, but after I enrolled, a bunch of servicemen came in on the G.I. Bill. Without the G.I. Bill, I'd have never gone to college.

In 1948, that fall, I was a senior. My wife-to-be, Mildred, happened to enroll as a freshman that year. And an odd thing about it was I was sitting outside the mess hall on a bench and I happened to see her, and her grandmother and mother were with her. I remembered her. But later on I met her through another couple, good friends of ours, and we had a double date with our friends. (Later on they got married, the friends, and we got married, too.)

I had a little car by that time. There were no cars made all during the war, but they made some in 1946. I guess that was the first year. I saw this little—I called it yellow, but it was a beige coupe. I had saved money while I was in the service and when I saw that car in Savannah, I went and bought it! I shouldn't have, but I did. So, I don't know if it was me or the car that Mildred liked the best.

We dated all the time that she was there. She took a one-year course. When she left Statesboro, she got a job at DuPont in Atlanta, and I decided to go on and get another degree. I don't know why. I only had the one undergraduate degree—it was a B.A. in education—so I went to Peabody College and got my Masters.

At that time Peabody was an independent college, but it was right across the street from Vanderbilt in Nashville, Tennessee. There were three colleges right together there: Vanderbilt, Peabody, and Scarrett College was just down the street. Peabody is a college for teachers. Now it's a college of education of Vanderbilt. So the three colleges had gone together and built one big library. The reason I mention that is because, going for a graduate degree, you have your own little desk in the library, so if I wanted to study, I'd just go to the library and get my little desk and turn on the light and study. This was a good arrangement for special study. I specialized in history.

Meanwhile, Mildred was back in Atlanta working for DuPont, and I just stayed in touch with her. I had my little car and did manage to get to Atlanta a couple of times. So, we decided to get married. One of my friends at Peabody—I had known him at Georgia Southern, but we got to know each other much better at Vanderbilt—I don't know how it came about now, but we decided to all get married at one time. He and his fiancée—her name was Mary Brinson—and Mildred all came to Nashville, and we got married in Nashville at a little Baptist church near Peabody. We had a double ceremony. Mildred's mother and grandmother came and the other couple's mother and sister came. We had a nice group there. It also included a good friend I'd made at Peabody (my roommate). He and his wife were there.

We took a honeymoon trip down off the coast of Georgia, on St. Simons Island. We spent several days there and then we had to come back to Atlanta. Mildred went back to work at DuPont. I had gotten a job with General Shoe Corporation, but in Chattanooga. I was selling shoes in a retail store. I worked up there for a while and she worked in Atlanta, and I came back and forth on the weekends, but that didn't work out! So I—with Mildred's permission—quit my job up there.

CHAPTER 14

A Man
Must
Work

Icame to Atlanta and I heard through the grapevine that Sears was hiring recent college graduates for their management training program. So I went by and talked with them, and they hired me. I guess probably what helped me get it was because I had an advanced degree.

At that time, Sears was located downtown on Ponce de Leon. The regional headquarters was there. At one time they had several thousand people working in that building. There's nothing there today. The city of Atlanta bought it. After a short training period, I was assigned to the regional buying office and became a buyer for the stores in the Southeast. I stayed in that job until I retired.

Over the years I bought several lines of merchandise: plumbing, carpet, window dressing, rugs. I was responsible for supplying merchandise for retail stores to sell. At one time, I was supplying merchandise not only to the retail stores, but to five catalog plants: Atlanta, Greensboro, Jacksonville, Memphis, and Dallas, Texas. I didn't have to do a whole lot of traveling because a lot of our contracts were made out of Chicago with parent buyers. They always came down and we traveled some together, but they were responsible for the master contracts.

At this point we were living in Atlanta. We lived in apartments called the Oakland Court Apartments near where the Atlanta Gas Light Company is now located, until we were able to buy our first house, which was in DeKalb County. It was a little three-bedroom, one-bath house. I think we moved in in 1952.

I stayed with Sears until I retired at the end of 1986. I had almost thirty-seven years of service, thirty-six and a half years. I stayed at this one job all those years, and a person might ask why I wasn't promoted to something else. Well, I had a family. The culture around Sears was that as long as you were a "yes" person, and you nodded your head like a puppet, oh, you were a fine man and you had the right attitude. Well, I learned that I wasn't that kind of person. If I had an idea that was different, I expressed it, and if they were doing something

I didn't particularly agree with, I'd say it. So I was pegged, I think, as having a poor attitude. It's a wonder, really, that I wasn't fired, but the fact is I kept that job for thirty-six and a half years. I did my best, and I managed.

G. C. and Mildred with Diane Lucile and Gregory Alan

CHAPTER 15

Offspring

But I'm getting ahead of myself. Mildred worked for DuPont, I worked for Sears Roebuck, and we bought a little house in Decatur on a street named Mark Trail. Our first child was born in 1957, August the 12th. A baby girl. We named her Barbara Maxine. Unfortunately, she lived only five weeks. She died of an extremely rare heart condition. When she was born, the pediatrician said she was in perfect health, but when she was about five weeks old, she suddenly got really ill one Sunday afternoon. The doctors at that time made house calls, believe it or not, so the pediatrician came out. He examined her and said we have to get her direct to the hospital immediately. She had this condition that he had never seen in his years of practice. He had studied about it in medical school and when he was interning; it was a condition called endocardial fibroelastosis. The inside lining of the heart loses its elasticity and becomes like leather. Of course the heart can't beat, and she died at five weeks old.

Before that, Mildred's first pregnancy resulted in a miscarriage of twins. So we had bad luck as far as that was concerned, but then, in 1958, our son was born—Greg, Gregory Allen—and he was fine. Of course, we were on edge all the time. And then just a year and a half later, our daughter Diane Lucile was born. Again we were on edge, but she was fine. And they brought much joy to our lives. And both have done very well.

They both graduated from Southeast DeKalb High School, and Greg became a drummer somewhere back along the line. He liked to play drums, and he took drum lessons from the time he was a little fellow until he got through high school. And he loved the marching band. So he decided he wanted to go to college at Jacksonville State University in Jacksonville, Alabama. They have an outstanding marching band. So he went to school over there and got his degree, and while he was there, he decided he wanted to study law. So he was accepted at Cumberland Law School at Samford University in Birmingham.

That's the Baptist school that's equivalent to Mercer, here. He got his degree there. And Diane went to the University of Georgia and graduated. She graduated Magna Cum Laude. She's done real well. Her major was Business Management.

Diane was married in 1985 and had one son, Josh Goodman. She and her husband divorced and she got custody of Josh. She had worked for Ford Motor Company, and while she worked there, she met Darryl Johnson. His father and he ran a Ford dealership outside of Athens in Crawford. She and Darryl were eventually married, and he helped raise Josh.

Greg married right after he got his law degree and passed the bar. Incidentally, he passed the bar on the first try. Very often you hear people taking the state bar several times, but he passed it the first time, and he married a girl that he went to high school with. They had two children, Erin and Alan, and they were divorced when Alan was about, oh, a year and a half old. He remarried, later, and had three more children, Madison, Garrett and Grant.

After Mildred and I moved down to McDonough, I went to a nearby cemetery, East Lawn Cemetery, and I bought three plots, and I had our daughter's grave moved here. (She was originally buried in a cemetery on the other side of Atlanta.) So she's right near where we can see her grave, put flowers on it.

G.C., Greg, Diane, and Mildred Futch, 1964

I had to see a licensed funeral director and he handled it for us. The other two are for me and my wife. We'll eventually end up down there.

Greg was the assistant district attorney in DeKalb County, and he decided he wanted to go into private practice. He heard this firm down here, Smith and Wells, wanted someone, so he interviewed with them and went with them. He was with them a while, but things didn't work out. He went back to being assistant district attorney in this circuit here for a while and then he decided to go out on his own. He opened his own law office down here in town, and he has done quite well.

Mildred and G. C., 1952 or 1953

CHAPTER 16

Life in Decatur

Mildred worked all the time our children were small. DuPont closed their offices here, and she could have transferred to Wilmington, Delaware, but we didn't want to do that. She took early retirement—I forgot what year that was, but it was before I retired. The children were in college by that time. She was with the company a long time. She worked for the paint division, which was a smaller division. Each division had a separate office around Atlanta. Her office was on Peachtree and North Avenue at one time, right near the Fox Theater. Wachovia had a bank underneath them. They were up over the bank. It could have been the building they imploded the other day. But they moved later out to North Atlanta, off of Elsworth, on Industrial Drive, and that's where they were when she retired.

Our address was Decatur, but we were not in the city of Decatur. We lived out in the county. It was fine. It was all right. It was a good place to live then. We did not live in the same house all the time. We moved. The little house we had was too small after the children came along, so we bought another house about two or three miles away. It was a much larger house. We lived there until we bought a house on Paddock Drive in a subdivision called Churchill Downs. That was near Southeast DeKalb High School, so they could go to school there. Again, our son, Greg, wanted to play in their band. They had an outstanding marching band. I guess if it hadn't been for the drums, he would probably never have gone to college. We moved to Summerland Drive and finally Paddock Drive, where we lived for some time.

We've always been Baptists, so for years we belonged to the Kirkwood Baptist Church. It moved from Kirkwood some years ago and moved out off Columbia Drive. I was ordained a deacon in 1969. Eventually, we moved our church membership from there out to a church called Smoke Rise Baptist Church. Now we're members at First Baptist Church of McDonough.

My parents were both Baptists. After they married, we

moved around so much. We weren't in one place long enough to go to a church to be affiliated with one. So, I didn't grow up in the church, but it was through Mildred's influence that we got back again. The pastor from the Kirkwood church, Paul Aiken, had our daughter's funeral. He was a real comfort to us; that was a trying time for both of us.

This was our first child when she died, and Dr. Julian Waters was her doctor. He asked us to come by his office one day after he had seen all of his patients. He had a long, long talk with us. He was probably fifteen years older than I, and he gave us a lot of things to think about. He encouraged us to go ahead and have another child quickly. There were only about fourteen months between her and when our son was born. And then there was only a year and a half when Diane came along. So, Mildred had three children in two years. Of course, we had trouble with a miscarriage.

Mildred's grandmother still was alive then—her grandmother Mercer. She lived here in Atlanta near Little Five Points. She had moved to Atlanta to take care of Mildred's great aunt. She spent most of her time caring for Mildred after the miscarriage. We stayed there with them—Mercer and Mildred's great aunt. It was near our apartment. They were real good to us. The great aunt died before our son was born, but she was still living when Mildred had the miscarriage. And so they told us to come up there where they could look after her because I had to work and Mildred got a leave of absence from her job.

CHAPTER 17

My Parents' Final Years

My parents moved to the farm on the Hall place and lived there for some time. Then my father purchased a two-acre site across the road and had a building moved there from Camp Stewart with the intention of living in one half and making a grocery store in the other part. He never did operate the store, but they did move there, perhaps 1951 or '52. By that time, his health began to fail, but he continued to work part-time whenever he could with my cousin Jack Shuman. Jack ran the Shuman Supply Company between Pembroke and Lanier. Finally in 1964, on or near my birthday, my father died suddenly of a heart attack. He is buried in the Northside

Esther Shuman Futch and Grover Cleveland Futch, Sr., in the early 1950s.

Cemetery in Pembroke.

My mother continued to live in Pembroke with Cecil, whose problems with alcohol continued. My sister Odell, whose husband had died sometime earlier, lived in Savannah and would come up on weekends to stay with her and help her out. As my mother advanced in age, Odell and her son moved to Pembroke to be nearer to her to help our mother.

My mother died in January of 1982. She is buried with my father and brother in the Northside Cemetery, where they had purchased lots some years before. After her death, her will was probated and carried out by Sam Pevey, who was the alternate named executor. (Mildred had been named as executor, but was unable to serve due to the fact that I had had a stroke when my mother was sick in the hospital.) The little place where my mother lived outside of town was sold. Cecil lived in an apartment near Odell in Pembroke, and lived there until he died in 1997. Buried now beside my parents are Alva, Cecil, Mary's son Freddie, and Odell.

CHAPTER 18

Ours Is Not to Reason Why

I'm a member of the VFW. I was a member of the American Legion for a time, and I'm also a member of the Veterans of the Battle of the Bulge, the SHAEF-ETOUSA Association (for World War II veterans who worked for General Eisenhower in Europe during the war), and the 12th Army Group Association. So many veterans of World War II are deceased now. We haven't had a reunion in several years. There are not enough of us left.

I was scheduled to go to the dedication of the World War II Memorial in Washington, D.C., but I was not physically able. The Veterans of the Battle of the Bulge was arranging for all the veterans who wanted to go to be there. They handled all the arrangements for us, and I was going to meet one old buddy that's still living in Florida. (Not Eddie, he's deceased.) My other close buddies from the service are deceased, except one. We lost contact for some time, but the 12th Army Group was having one of their reunions and I got a roster and saw his name on there.

From left, G. C. Futch, Ed Gay, H.M. Fulbright, and Perlie Brantley, about 1948

He was living in Gainesville, Florida, even though originally he was from upstate New York. So we got in touch with each other. I've been down to see him once since we reestablished contact with each other. We keep in touch now by phone and Christmas cards and things like that. But he's the only one left. He is now eighty-nine years old. All the others are gone.

I had one buddy who was from Salt Lake City, that area, but he's gone. And the other one that I worked real close with in my office in the 12th Army Group was from Hinkley, Minnesota. I called him one time when I found out the 12th Army Group was going to have a reunion down this way to see if he could come. I talked to his wife, and found he had died the year before and I didn't know it. I knew her because she was an English girl from London, and while we were in Verdun, he got permission to go back to London to marry her. I still have their wedding picture. I talked to her and she thought that she and her son might come to one of our reunions, but they never did. You know, once that long a period of time has elapsed, it's just hard to renew any kind of a relationship.

Of course, I kept in touch with Eddie. He went into teaching and he taught in several places in Georgia. He was a school superintendent and a school principal for a while. Before the last time I saw him, another friend called me and said, "Did you know that Eddie has cancer?"

"No, I didn't," I said. Then he gave me Eddie's current phone number, and I called him. He was living in Warner Robins.

First, I went by myself to see him at his home. He was not too sick at that time, and we got to reminisce and talk for several hours, and then I drove back up. But then later I heard he was in the hospital in Warner Robins, so Mildred and I went one Sunday morning, drove down and visited him in the hospital. He wasn't doing well.

We came back home, and it's about that time that I had a stroke—a cerebral hemorrhage—and while I was confined here, he died. So I didn't get to see him anymore. I'd known him since we were about eight or nine, ten years old. We did a lot of things together growing up. We went fishing together and camping. We camped out by the river one time, a couple of days. Of course, that got to be old pretty quickly and we went home rather suddenly. We left our tent. We packed everything up, and left it. We walked back in to town and my dad went down in his old flivver and picked the thing up.

The fellow in Florida is the only one I know from my really distant past. I have one relative, the great-granddaughter that my grandmother Shuman raised, who's still living, but she's got Alzheimer's. All the others of my cousins are all deceased. I have only one sister left, my younger sister. All my brothers and sisters and my parents are deceased.

G. C. and Mildred on their 50th wedding anniversary, June 2000

I had two brothers and four sisters. There were three boys and four girls. Well, really there were five girls, counting the one that died as an infant. We're all gone now except me and my younger sister. And incidentally, I just had my 82nd birthday. She and I have the same birthday: September the 16th, exactly two years apart. So my daughter, Diane – she was up to it again – called long distance to my sister's daughter-in-law and arranged for them to come to see me on that Sunday. They had a little party for me here in secret. I didn't even know she was coming until she walked in the door. I had not seen her for four years! (We don't drive much anymore.) She lives in Pembroke, where I grew up. She's the only one still living. So, time marches on.

I've often wondered why I was able to live this long, and be blessed the way I've been blessed. I don't know why. But I guess I don't have to know why.

I've always liked a line from "The Charge of the Light Brigade," and I'd like to close my story with it: "Ours is not to reason why, ours is but to do or die." And so it goes.

INDEX

A

B

D

Dallas, Texas 66

Dania, Florida 15

Davis, President Jefferson 10

DeKalb County, Georgia 66, 73

Depression, Great Depression 23, 24, 26, 31

Dietrich, Marlene 50

Downs, Mary 8

    Billie (Uncle Billie) 8

Downs Town, Georgia 2, 5, 26

Dresden, Germany 8

Duggar place 26

DuPont 62, 63, 64, 69, 75

E

Eagle Main 57

Eagle Tac 57

East Lawn Cemetery 71

Eiffel Tower 56

Eisenhower, General Dwight D. 38, 51, 53, 82

Emory Smith place 23

Endocardial Fibroelastosis 70

ETOUSA (European Theater of Operations, U. S. Army) 53

F

R

S

www.ingramcontent.com/pod-product-compliance
Lightning Source LLC
Chambersburg PA
CBHW030759150426
42813CB00068B/3267/J